Start Right Reader

GRADE 2 · BOOK 1

Printed in the U.S.A.

ISBN   978-1-328-70201-2

7 8 9 10   0928   26 25 24 23 22 21

4500825774   B C D E F G

Contents

Week 1

Week 2

Week 3

Get Started

Meet Kim and Dan. Kim and Dan like fig jam.
What happens when Kim and Dan run out of jam?
Read to find out!

Kim

Dan

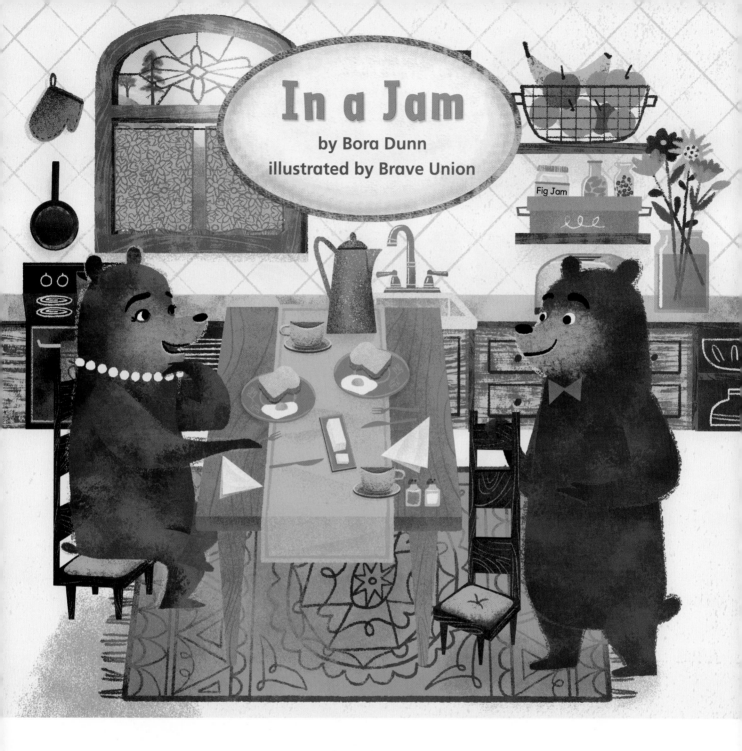

In a Jam

by Bora Dunn

illustrated by Brave Union

Kim and Dan sat.

"Will you have jam, Kim? It is fig jam."

"I will have jam, Dan."

"Sit, Kim, sit. I will go. It is in the bin."

Dan got the fig jam.
Kim is sad. It has not got a bit in it.
"Dig in it, Kim. Can you nab a bit?"
Kim can not.

Kim will tip the jam and tap it. Kim can not
nab the jam.

"I dip and dip, Dan. I hit it. I tip it. I tap it.
Jam is not in it. I can not have jam."

Dan is sad.

"Max has fig jam, Kim. I will go to Max."
Dan got his bag. Dan ran to Max.
Dan got jam, a yam, and wax in a can. It
can fit in his big tan bag.

"I got the jam. Kim can have fig jam!"

Dan ran. Dan can zip to his pal Kim.

Dan had the big tan bag. It hit his hip as Dan ran.

"Kim! I am the man! I have fig jam! Dig in the big tan bag!"

Kim got the wax in a can. Kim got the yam.

Fig jam? It is not in the bag!

"Dan, the bag has a big rip in it."

Kim did not have fig jam. Dan is mad.

Story Captions

Take turns reading these words to a partner.

a	and	go	got	have
not	the	to	you	will

Write about the picture. Choose words
from the box, or use your own words
to complete each sentence.

1. Dan **and** Kim do **not have** ____.

2. Dan **will go to** ____.

3. Dan **got** ____.

Read your sentences to a partner.

Blend and Read

1. pat   hip   hat   pit   nip   catnip

2. cab   can   quit   attic   fib   zigzag

3. am   six   man   pin   fit   hatpin

4. nap   visit   sat   bag   big   picnic

5. magic   panic   timid   valid   rapid

6. Kim dips and digs in the jam.

7. Kim, you can not have jam.

8. Dan can fit the jam in his big bag.

Jam Bandit

by Bora Dunn

illustrated by Brave Union

Rabbit has a mat. Rabbit has a bag.
Rabbit and Cat will have a big picnic.
"I can go to Cat. Cat and I can gab at the
big picnic."

Rabbit is at the pit.

"Is it jam? It is! It is fig jam. It can fit in the bag. Cat can have jam at the picnic."

Rabbit ran to Cat.

Rabbit and Cat sat at the mat.

"Have the fig jam, Cat."

Rabbit got Cat a napkin. Cat can have a napkin as a bib.

Is it in a bin? Is it in a gap? It is not.
Kim can not have fig jam.

"I did have fig jam, Kim. I did! I did!
I am mad."

"It is Rabbit! Rabbit has the jam!"
Dan and Kim ran at Rabbit.

"Rabbit, you have fig jam. It is the jam I got! I am mad at you, Rabbit!"

Rabbit is sad. Cat is sad.

"Dan, Rabbit is not bad. The bag had a rip in it. Rabbit is not a jam bandit. Rabbit is a pal."

"Dan, I got the jam in the pit. Dan, Kim, sit, sit. Sit and gab! It is a picnic, Dan. You and Kim can fit at the mat."

Dan sat. Kim sat. Kim had fig jam. Dan, Rabbit, and Cat dig in to fig jam. The picnic is a big hit!

Show What You Know

Reread both stories to answer these questions.

1. What problem do Kim and Dan have in **In a Jam**? What does Dan do to solve it?

2. What event in **In a Jam** leads to Kim and Dan joining Rabbit and Cat at the picnic?

3. Is Rabbit a jam bandit? Why or why not? Use details from **Jam Bandit** in your answer.

Talk about your answers with a partner.

Get Started

In these stories, Dad, Ken, and Max get an old van. It does not go.

Will they get the van to go? Where might they go in the van? Will Mom like it? Read to find out!

Dad

Ken

Max

Mom

The Red Van

by Molly Davis

illustrated by Talitha Shipman

Dad, Ken, and Max get a red van. The van has gas, but it does not run.

"It is a sad van, Dad! It is on, but it cannot run, and it has mud on it!"

"It is not a bad van, Ken. It is not sad. I can fix it. I can get it to run."

Dad does the job. The van can run.

Ken can see the job Dad did. "Not bad, Dad! You got it to hum."

Max can see the job Dad did. "Not bad, Dad!"

"I left you a big job, men. It is the best job.
The van has mud on it. You can wash the van."
Max got a rag. Ken got a tub and a rag.
Ken and Max wash the red van.

It is hot in the sun, but Ken and Max dig in.
Ken had fun on the job. Max had fun. Dad got
wet! Max and Ken had more fun than Dad did.

Ken and Max wash the red van, end to end.
Ken and Max rub wax on it. It is fun!

Dad does not see mud. Dad can see the job
Max and Ken did. "Not bad, men! It is not a
sad van, Ken."

Ken got Mom. Mom got in the van. Dad,
Max, and Ken got in.

Mom sat up in the van. Mom hit the gas.
The van has pep! It can go. Hit it, Mom!

Secret Word Game

 Play with a partner.
Use a timer. Take turns.

than	best	end	job	left
men	does	wash	see	more

1. Think of a word in the box.

2. Set the timer.

3. Tell a clue about the word.

4. Your partner tries to guess the secret word.

5. Continue until your partner guesses or time runs out.

The first to guess five secret words wins!

Blend and Read

1. ten   pen   sunset   puppet   run   lot

2. dug   leg   velvet   magnet   dog   sun

3. cat   fan   napkin   catnap   hit   limit

4. bat   man   rabbit   picnic   habit   bin

5. jut   lag   absent   dentist   ticket   trim

6. Did Dad get the van to run?

7. Dad left Ken and Max a fun job.

8. Ken and Max wash and wax the van.

Picnic Fun

by Molly Davis

illustrated by Talitha Shipman

Mom, Dad, Ken, and Max will go on a picnic. Mom set a big mat and a picnic basket in the van. Dad has a map in his lap.

Mom, Dad, Ken, and Max left to go on the picnic.

"Mom! Dad! Is it a cactus? It is red on top.
Can I go see it?"

"In a bit, Max. Sit on the mat. Ken, get
Max a cup." Ken got it.

Ken and Max sat on the mat. Max had a sip.
Ken and Mom had a hot dog on a bun. Max
had a hot dog but left his bun.   Dad did not
get a hot dog. Dad had jam on a bun.

Max ran on to the cactus. Ken got up and
ran to Max. Ken got up on a big log.

"Max! I can see a kitten! It is in a gap in the
log. I can get it. It can fit in a cap! Mom! Dad!"

Ken sat on the log. The kitten got up and sat
in his cap. Mom will get it.

"Pat it, Max! Mom, it is a kitten! It is a pet.
It is sad."

"Yes, Ken, it is a pet. Dad has a box in the
van. Dad can get it to a vet."

"Can it go in the van, Mom?"

"Yes, Max, it can."

Ken let the kitten nap in his box. The kitten
is more fun than the picnic. Ken let Max pat it.
Dad and Mom will let Max and Ken have it
as a pet. It is the best pet!

What If?

Reread both stories. Then write your answers to these questions.

1. What if Dad did not get the van to run? How might the stories be different?

2. How would **Picnic Fun** be different if Ken saw a wild animal and not a kitten?

3. What if **you** lost your kitten? What would you do to find it?

Share your answers with a group.

Get Started

Meet Zane, a rabbit. He will hike to Lime Lake. Watch out for the fox, Zane!

What will Kevin Fox do to stop Zane? How will Pip help Zane get to Lime Lake? Read to find out!

Zane   Pip   Kevin

Zane on a Hike

by Axel Rocha
illustrated by Katie Kath

"I like to hike," Zane said. "I can hike a mile. I can make it to Lime Lake. I can have a fine picnic in the sun."

Zane got his hat, his map, and his bag. He got his picnic basket. Zane is set.

Zane is in the lane. His pal Pip is on a red bike. Pip has on a velvet cape.

Zip! Pip can ride in the lane. The lane is not wide, but Zane can hop to the side. Zane and Pip wave. Zane will hike on to Lime Lake.

Zane came upon a wide pen. It had a gate.
A big pine hid a fox den.

"I see Kevin Fox!" Zane said. "His den is in
the pine. Kevin Fox is not a pal to a rabbit."

A fox can bite a rabbit like Zane. Kevin can dine on Zane! Can Zane run? Can Zane hide? Zane can see Lime Lake, but he cannot dig a tunnel to it. Can he get to his picnic at Lime Lake?

Kevin Fox came to his gate.

"Can I walk in the pen to get to Lime Lake, Kevin?" Zane said. "It will save time, and I am late."

"Sure, Zane," Kevin said. "I can let you hike in the pen, but I will make you do a job."

Zane got pale. He bit his lip. Can he do the job Zane will give him?

Will Zane quit? Can Zane get to his picnic at Lime Lake?

Use That Word

Take turns. Play with a friend until you use all the words.

line	set	walk	sure	seven
upon	give	said	he	do

1. Pick a word and read it.

2. Your friend uses the word in a sentence.

3. Then your friend picks a word and reads it.

4. You use your friend's word in a sentence.

Blend and Read

1. cape   kite   tape   bite   bake   bike

2. cage   rice   race   page   mice   face

3. tub   vet   mitten   set   sob   attic

4. but   button   kitten   kit   rib   ribbon

5. grate   vane   spine   brave   prime   crane

6. Zane can walk a mile to Lime Lake.

7. Pip rides a bike in the lane.

8. Kevin has a den in a nice, wide pen.

Six Fake Mice

by Axel Rocha

illustrated by Katie Kath

Zane ran to his pal Pip.

"Kevin Fox said I have to give him seven fat mice," Zane said. "If I do not get him the mice, I cannot walk in his pen. I will not get to Lime Lake."

"Bad fox!" Pip said. "I can fix him, Zane!"

Pip got the velvet cape and cut it up. Zane gave Pip tape and a button.

Pip gave Zane a pen and a pencil. Zane made a face on the velvet.

Pip and Zane made six fake mice.

Zane set the fake mice in a cage. Pip got in the cage. Pip and the six fake mice sat in a line. Zane had seven mice in the line!

"Zane, take us to Kevin Fox," Pip said. "Fox will get a big lesson!"

"Zane is at the gate," Kevin said. "He has a cage. Zane has mice. Yum! I can dine on nice fat mice—and on a rabbit!"

Kevin gave Zane a wave. He ran to the gate.

Zane gave Kevin the cage. Pip gave the six
fake mice a tap. The fake mice gave a hop.
Kevin made a dive.

"Run, Zane!" Pip said.

"Fake mice!" Kevin said in a rage.

Kevin ran at Zane and Pip, but a rabbit like Zane can race!

Kevin quit. "I give up," Kevin said. "I am not sure I like mice. I will take a nap."

Zane and Pip had a nice picnic at Lime Lake. Kevin Fox sat in his pen.

Story Details

Reread both stories. Then answer the questions.

1. What does Zane want to do?

2. What problem does Zane have?

3. What does Pip do to help Zane?

4. Does Kevin Fox really like to eat mice?
    Give reasons for your answer.

Talk about your answers with a group.

Get Started

Meet Cat. Cat is a lone cat. He is on his own in the world. Then Cat finds June and Pete. Will they become pals?

Will June and Pete give Cat a home? Who is Duke? Read to find out!

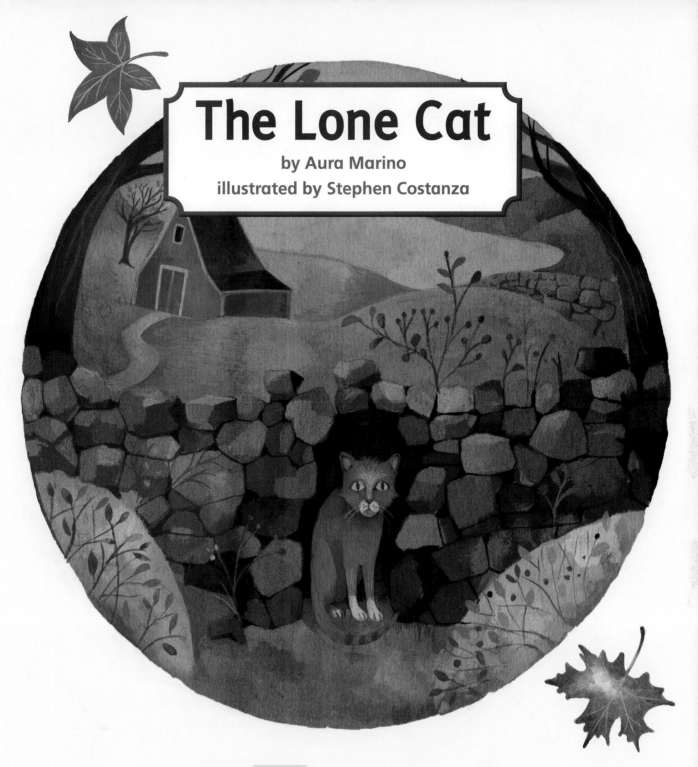

The Lone Cat

by Aura Marino

illustrated by Stephen Costanza

Cat has no name. He has no pal. Cat is a lone cat.

It is cold. Cat has a den in a tunnel. It is close to a lake, but a tunnel is not a home. Cat does not have a nice life. Cat has hope he can get to a fine home.

Cat ran on the lane. He ran a mile and came up to a gate. Cat can see a home. He can see a man in it. The man got a log. He set the log on a big, hot fire.

Cat ran on to the home, the man, and the fire.

At sunset, Cat came up to the home.
He sat at the front. The home had a big rug
close to the big, hot fire.

"June! I can see a cat," the man said.

"It is cute, Pete, but it is no kitten,"
said June.

Cat can see in the home. He can see
the fire.

Pete came up to Cat to pat him, but Cat did not let him. Cat did not like it. Cat gave Pete a small nip.

"Rude cat," Pete said.

"The cat is not nice," June said. "It is not tame. It is not safe. It cannot come in."

The sun rose. A rabbit came up to the gate. It made a hole. It dug in a pot. It ate a bite.

"Bad rabbit!" Pete said. Pete is mad at the rabbit. Cat ran at the rabbit. The rabbit hid in a small hole.

"Nice job, Cat," Pete said.

Pete came up to Cat and sat. Cat let Pete sit
at his side. He let Pete pat him. Cat did not
hate it! Cat got up on Pete and sat in his lap.
Pete gave Cat a pat.

June gave Cat a pat. "In time, if he is tame,
we can let him in," June said.

Story Word Hunt

Read the words below to a partner.

come	close	name	fire	life
times	done	front	cold	small

1. Together, look for each word in a story sentence. Write the words you find. What words were **not** there?

2. Write two words that you did not see in the story. Write sentences for the words. Read your sentences to your partner.

Blend and Read

1. Pete be tube robe no music

2. woke make mule bake cute rule

3. page nice age rapid pen pencil

4. lace rice life race but button

5. broke even flute stone flu space

6. Did Cat get mud on his front leg?

7. Will June let Cat come in the home?

8. Can Cat sit on the rug close to the fire?

Cat Has a Pal

by Aura Marino

illustrated by Stephen Costanza

Cat has a pal. His pal is Pete! Pete can pat Cat. Cat will nap in his lap. Cat is not a lone cat, but he does not have a home yet.

June and Pete have a nice home, but Cat does not go inside. It is not his home yet, but will it be?

"Can the cat come in?" Pete said. "It is cold."

"I am not sure, Pete. He bit you," June said. "He is not tame. He is not a pet. I am not sure he can come inside yet."

June and Pete had a hot fire, but Cat did not. Cat is cold and sad.

Cat can nap in a big box, but a box is not like a home. A wide tub is nice to nap in, but it is not a home. Cat can nap in a basket. The basket is not bad, but it has a hole. Cat is so cold!

Cat came up to the home. He can see the big, hot fire.

Cat sat up. Mice! His nose led him to the mice. Cat dove at the mice. Mice came up to him more times, but Cat ran at the mice.

"No mice!" Pete said. "Cat has done the job. It is time we let him in. He can have a life inside."

Inside, Cat can see a button. It is red.
Cat gave the button a poke. Cat made it hop.
He gave it a tap. He dove at it.

June gave the button a poke to see Cat dive
at it. June, Pete, and Cat had fun.

"He is cute!" said June.

"I like the cat," June said. "He is tame.
He is a pet. We can give him a name. We can
name him Duke."

"Done!" Pete said. "Duke it is!"

Duke came in and sat. He had a nap. He is
not a lone cat. He has a name. He is home.

Characters

Reread both stories. Then look at the pictures.

1. Talk with a partner about which character you think changes the most. Use details in the stories to support your thinking.

2. On a sheet of paper, write about your favorite character. Write why that one is your favorite. Share your work with your partner.

Get Started

Meet Miss Pam's class. They are playing the Bag Game.

What is the Bag Game? What does Miss Pam have in the bag? What will the kids bring to Miss Pam's class? Read to find out!

Game Time

by Ian Costas

illustrated by Margeaux Lucas

I am Rose. I like the Bag Game! What is in the big bag? We cannot see until we quiz Miss Pam to find the answer.

"Is it as big as the bag?" Nate said.

"No, Nate," Miss Pam said, "but it is not as small as a dime."

"Can we take it on a picnic?" Eve said. "Is it a napkin? Is it a cup?"

"No, Eve," Miss Pam said. "It is not a napkin. It is not a cup."

Then Eve said, "Is it cake? I hope so! Yum! Did you bake us a nice big cake?"

"No, Eve," Miss Pam said. "I like cake, but I did not bake a cake!"

"I bet it is a kite," Dom said. No, it is not.

"Did you dig up an old bone?" I said.

"No, Rose. It is not a bone, but it is old," Miss Pam said. "It is as old as I am."

We quiz Miss Pam a bit more. It is not
round, but it is not a cube. It is not hot, but it is
not cold like ice. It is cute. It is tan. It is fun.
It can fit in a box. It has a hole in it.

"Give us the answer!" we beg.

Miss Pam cannot. It is the rule!

"Has it got a nose?" Mike said.

"Yes, it has!" Miss Pam said.

"A man has a nose," said Mike. "Did you hide a man in the bag?"

"Nice joke, Mike, but it is not a man!" Miss Pam said.

"Is it a cat?" I said. "Is it a fox?"

"Close, Rose!" Miss Pam said. "It is a dog.
His name is Mel. I got Mel as a kid. He is old,
but he is mine and I like him. Did you like the
Bag Game?"

"Yes, yes!" we rave.

Letter Mix-Up

Read the words below to a partner.

until	round	miss	what	then
answer	young	old	find	its

Oh, no! The letters in the words got mixed up!
Work with your partner. Put the letters in order
to spell a word in the box.

1. i s t

2. d o l

3. i f d n

4. s m s i

5. g u y o n

6. a w t h

7. u r d n o

8. t u l i n

9. s a w e r n

10. n e t h

Blend and Read

1. attic   picnic   coldest   colder   older   oldest

2. tape   nice   smallest   smaller   tablet   kitten

3. pet   Pete   cub   cube   rob   robe

4. pan   pane   dim   dime   dome   dine

5. pike   pave   mane   mole   fame   vane

6. Rose will like the Bag Game.

7. I hope Miss Pam made a nice cake.

8. Mel is older than Mike and Dom.

Big Hen, Old Fox

by Ian Costas

illustrated by Margeaux Lucas

Nate has a big dog. His mom made it.
Its name is Tip. Tip is a fine dog, but he is
quite old. His leg has a hole.

Rose has Fox, a big puppet. It is cute and
red. Fox is older than Tip.

"Dad had Fox as a kid," Rose said.

Mike has Hen. His dad got Hen at a sale and gave it to Mike. It is not old. Hen is as big as a kid!

Eve has Rabbit. It has a fat red rose, a lace cap, and a basket. Its nose is a big dot on its face.

Dom has Red Cat. It is a puppet like Fox.
Red Cat can fit like a mitten. Dom can make
Red Cat nod and wave at Fox.

Red Cat is like Fox, but it is not the same
size as Fox. Red Cat is smaller.

Big

Smallest

Youngest

Oldest

"Hen is as big as Mike!" Miss Pam said.
"We can make a size line. Then we can go
young to old."

Tip is smaller than Hen. Rabbit and Fox
are the same size. The smallest is Red Cat.
Hen is youngest. Fox is oldest.

"We can make up a tale," Miss Pam said. "What can happen in it?"

"Fox and Red Cat can have a fun picnic," Dom said. "Tip and Rabbit can race."

"Hen can go up in a big jet and take Red Cat on a ride," Mike said.

"We can have Mel, Fox, Tip, Rabbit, and Hen hike up a hill," Rose said. "Hen can use a rope to get Red Cat to the top. It is a mile up to the summit!"

It is time to vote. What tale will it be?
The vote is close. Did Rose win? Yes!

Think-Write-Pair-Share

Reread the stories. Think and then write answers to these questions.

1. What does Miss Pam put in the big bag?
   If **you** were Miss Pam, what would you put in the bag?

2. What are two ways that Miss Pam's class sorts their animals?

3. In her tale, why does Rose choose Hen to help Red Cat get to the hilltop?

Share your work with a partner and then in a group.

Get Started

You will be reading about many kinds of birds. What do you know about birds?

How do mom and dad birds take care of their young? Can a bird be as big as a man? Can a bird be as small as an ice cube? Read to find out!

Not Yet

by Alma Sims

I am a baby bird. I can sit. I can beg to be fed, but I cannot fly yet. I cannot go get a bug, but Mom can. She can fly.

Mom can nab a big fat bug on a stem and bring it home to me. I sit until I see Mom fly up. Did Mom get a bug? I get the best bug!

Tap! Tap! Tap! Mom can tap to get us a bug. She can make a hole and poke in it to get a bug. Get it, Mom! Mom can fly and take the bug to us at home.

Home is a hole. We sit in the hole. It is a safe place. Mom came! Give us a bug, Mom!

I cannot fly yet, but I can flap. I can nip. I can beg Mom and Dad to go get mice.

Mom can glide and get me nice, fat mice. Mom will then take the mice home. I grab and snap up the mice. I do not stop. Yum, mice! When I am big, I can go get mice.

I am a baby crane. I cannot fly yet, but I can walk. I trot to be close to Mom and Dad.

I am not a big crane, and I cannot fly yet, but I can grab a bug. I can get a grip on a fat frog. I can poke at mice and snag a small snake. I am glad I am fed.

I am in a big place. I cannot fly yet, but I can snap and nip at you. Do not get close!

Mom can glide like a plane. Mom can dine on what is left on an old bone. Mom will snip, bite, and tug at it. Mom will take a bit home to me! This is what I like! Mom is the best!

I am in a cold place. It is home to me. I cannot fly. Mom and Dad cannot fly, but Mom and Dad can swim.

I cannot swim yet, but I will get big. I will swim, dive, and dip like Mom and Dad. I will slip and slide on ice. I will zip on ice in no time!

Story Break

Read this story with a partner.

1. **This little bird** cannot **fly** up in the **blue** yet.

2. **She** is a **baby** and cannot get a bug.

3. She will sit in **her** safe **place**.

4. Mom bird will **bring** her a bug.

5. "Give me **this** bug, Mom. Yum!"

Role-play with your partner. One can be the mom bird and the other can be the baby bird. Take turns being mom and baby.

Blend and Read

1. drip   grapes   stop   flops   drives   bliss

2. slots   boxes   bran   mixes   snap   trips

3. rose   sudden   rule   fame   tale   lesson

4. kitten   button   fire   mitten   pile   reptile

5. ramp   stamp   rest   crest   craft   blast

6. The blue bird can snag the big bug.

7. Mom bird can glide and snap up mice.

8. A baby crane can poke, grab, and grip.

Big and Small

by Alma Sims

Birds come in sizes big and small. This bird is quite big. It is as big as a man. It cannot fly, but it can run!

Dad and his baby birds go on walks. The birds snap up bugs, buds, and slugs. Yum!

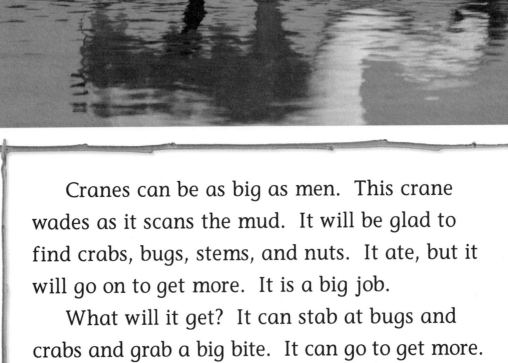

Cranes can be as big as men. This crane wades as it scans the mud. It will be glad to find crabs, bugs, stems, and nuts. It ate, but it will go on to get more. It is a big job.

What will it get? It can stab at bugs and crabs and grab a big bite. It can go to get more.

This bird is not as big as a crane. It can fly, but it likes to run! If it sees a snake, it runs at it and grabs it. It can dine on snakes, bugs, and reptiles. It dines on what it can get.

It is at home in a hot place. You can find pale foxes, bats, bugs, and big cactuses in this place.

This bird is blue. He is quite little. He has spots on his face. He is a pet. A kid is his pal. His kid pal gave him the name Dot. Dot is cute!

Dot makes his home in a nice, big cage. He likes it in his cage. He can hop and flit in it. He has fun in his cage.

This blue bird is not a pet. It is not big. Mom gets big bugs to bring to her baby birds. Her little birds like big, fat bugs. Mom has a big job.

Birds can use boxes as homes. The box has a hole in it. Baby birds can sit inside it. It is a safe place. Moms and dads can go in it.

This bird is not big. It is the same size as an ice cube!

It can flit, zip, zig, and zag. It can stop in place as it sips at buds. It sips and it zips on. It makes a hum as it zips and flits.

K-W-L Chart

Reread the texts. Make a chart to show what you have learned about birds.

Birds		
K	**W**	**L**
What I **K**now	What I **W**ant to Know	What I **L**earned

Talk about your work with a group.

WORD LISTS

* = High-Frequency Word

BOOK 1 **In a Jam** p. 5

■ Decodable Words

TARGET SKILLS: *Consonants; Short* a, i

am*, as*, bag, big*, bin, bit, can*, Dan, did*, dig, dip, fig, fit, had*, has*, hat, hip, his*, hit, in*, is*, it*, jam, Kim, mad, man*, Max, nab, pal, ran*, rip, sad, sat*, sit*, tan, tap, tip, wax, yam, zip

PREVIOUSLY TAUGHT

I*

■ High-Frequency Words
NEW

a, and, go, got, have, not, the, to, will, you

BOOK 2 **Jam Bandit** p. 13

■ Decodable Words

TARGET SKILLS: *Consonants; Short* a, i; *Multisyllabic Words: Short* a, i

am*, as*, at*, bad*, bag, bandit, bib, big*, bin, can*, cat, Dan, did*, dig, fig, fit, gab, had*, has*, hit, in*, is*, it*, jam, Kim, mad, mat, napkin, pal, picnic, pit, rabbit, ran*, rip, sad, sat*, sit*

PREVIOUSLY TAUGHT

I*

■ High-Frequency Words
NEW

a, and, go, got, have, not, the, to, will, you

WORD LISTS

* = High-Frequency Word

BOOK 1 **The Red Van** p. 21

■ Decodable Words

TARGET SKILLS: *Consonants; Short* o, u, e

but*, cannot*, fun*, get*, got*, hot*, hum, Ken, mom, mud, not*, on*, pep, red*, rub, run*, sun*, tub, up*, wet

PREVIOUSLY TAUGHT SKILLS

bad*, big*, can*, dad, did*, dig, fix, gas, had*, has*, hit*, I*, in*, is*, it*, Max, rag, sad, sat*, van, wax

■ High-Frequency Words
NEW

best, does, end, job, left, men, more, see, than, wash

PREVIOUSLY TAUGHT

a, and, go, the, to, you

BOOK 2 **Picnic Fun** p. 29

■ Decodable Words

TARGET SKILLS: *Consonants; Short* o, u, e; *Multisyllabic Words: Short* o, u, e

basket, box, bun, but*, cactus, cup, dog, fun*, get*, got*, hot*, Ken, kitten, let*, log, mom, not*, on*, pet, red*, set*, top, up*, vet, yes*

PREVIOUSLY TAUGHT SKILLS

as*, big*, bit, can*, cap, dad, did*, fit, gap, had*, has*, his*, I*, in*, is*, it*, jam, lap, map, mat, Max, nap, pat, picnic, ran*, sad, sat*, sip, sit*, van

■ High-Frequency Words
NEW

best, left, more, see, than

PREVIOUSLY TAUGHT

a, and, go, have, the, to, will

* = High-Frequency Word

BOOK 1 **Zane on a Hike** p. 37

■ Decodable Words
TARGET SKILL: *Long* a, i *(VCe)*

bike, bite, came*, cape, dine, fine, gate, hide, hike, lake, lane, late, like*, lime, make*, mile, pale, pine, ride*, save, side*, time*, wave, wide, Zane

PREVIOUSLY TAUGHT SKILLS

am*, at*, bag, basket, big*, bit, but*, can*, cannot*, den, dig, fox, get*, got*, had*, has*, hat, hid, him*, his*, hop, I*, in*, is*, it*, job, Kevin, let*, lip, map, not*, on*, pal, pen, picnic, Pip, quit, rabbit, red*, run*, sun*, tunnel, velvet, zip

■ High-Frequency Words
NEW

do, give, he, said, set, sure, upon, walk

PREVIOUSLY TAUGHT

a, and, have, see, the, to, will, you

BOOK 2 **Six Fake Mice** p. 45

■ Decodable Words
TARGET SKILLS: *Long* a, i *(VCe); Soft* c *and* g

cage, cape, dine, dive, face, fake, gate, gave, lake, like*, lime, made*, mice, nice, race, rage, take*, tape, wave, Zane

PREVIOUSLY TAUGHT SKILLS

am*, at*, bad*, big*, but*, button, can*, cannot*, cut*, fat*, fix, fox, get*, got*, had*, has*, him*, his*, hop, I*, if*, in*, is*, it*, Kevin, lesson, nap, not*, on*, pal, pen, pencil, picnic, Pip, quit, rabbit, ran*, run*, sat*, six, tap, up*, us*, velvet, yum

■ High-Frequency Words
NEW

do, give, he, line, said, set, seven, sure, walk

PREVIOUSLY TAUGHT

a, and, have, the, to, will

* = High-Frequency Word

BOOK 1 **The Lone Cat** p. 53

■ Decodable Words

TARGET SKILL: *Long o, e, u (CV, VCe)*

cute, hole, home*, hope, June, lone, no*, Pete, rose, rude

PREVIOUSLY TAUGHT SKILLS

at*, ate*, bad*, big*, bite, but*, came*, can*, cannot*, cat, den, did*, dug, fine, gate, gave*, get*, got*, had*, has*, hate, he*, hid, him*, his*, hot*, I*, if*, in*, is*, it*, job, kitten, lake, lane, lap, let*, like*, log, mad, made*, man*, mile, nice, nip, not*, on*, pal, pat, pot, rabbit, ran*, rug, safe, sat*, set*, side*, sit*, sun*, sunset, tame, time*, tunnel, up*, we*

■ High-Frequency Words

NEW

close, cold, come, fire, front, life, name, small

PREVIOUSLY TAUGHT

a, and, does, have, said, see, the, to

BOOK 2 **Cat Has a Pal** p. 61

■ Decodable Words

TARGET SKILLS: *Long o, e, u (CV, VCe); Review Long Vowels (VCe)*

be*, came*, cute, dive, dove, Duke, gave*, go*, he*, hole, home*, inside*, June, like*, lone, made*, mice, nice, no*, nose, Pete, poke, so*, tame, we*, wide

PREVIOUSLY TAUGHT SKILLS

am*, at*, bad*, basket, big*, bit, box, but*, button, can*, cat, did*, fun*, had*, has*, him*, his*, hop, hot*, I*, in*, is*, it*, job, lap, led, let*, nap, not*, pal, pat, pet, ran*, red*, sad, sat*, tap, tub, up*, yet*

■ High-Frequency Words

NEW

cold, come, done, fire, life, name, time, times

PREVIOUSLY TAUGHT

a, and, does, give, have, more, said, see, sure, the, to, will, you

BOOK 1 **Game Time** p. 69

■ Decodable Words

TARGET SKILLS: *Short and Long Vowels (CVC, VCe)*

bag, bake, beg, bet, big*, bit, bone, box, but*, cake, can*, cannot*, cat, cube, cup, cute, did*, dig, dime, dog, Dom, Eve, fit, fox, fun*, game, got*, has*, hide, him*, his*, hole, hope, hot*, joke, kid, ice, kite, like*, man*, Mel, Mike, mine, name*, napkin, Nate, nice, nose, not*, Pam, picnic, quiz, rave, Rose, rule, take*, tan, time*, yes*, yum

PREVIOUSLY TAUGHT SKILLS

am*, an*, as*, he*, I*, in*, is*, it*, no*, on*, so*, up*, us*, we*

■ High-Frequency Words
NEW

answer, find, miss, old, round, then, until, what

PREVIOUSLY TAUGHT

a, and, close, cold, give, more, said, see, small, the, to, you

BOOK 2 **Big Hen, Old Fox** p. 77

■ Decodable Words

TARGET SKILLS: *Short and Long Vowels (CVC, VCe);*
   Suffixes -er, -est

basket, big*, but*, can*, cap, cat, cute, dad, did*, dog, Dom, dot, Eve, face, fat*, fine, fit, fox, fun*, gave*, get*, got*, had*, happen*, has*, hen, hike, his*, hole, jet, kid, lace, leg, like*, line*, made*, make*, Mel, Mike, mile, mitten, mom, name*, Nate, nod, nose, not*, older, oldest, Pam, picnic, puppet, quite, rabbit, race, red*, ride*, rope, rose, sale, same*, size, smaller, smallest, summit, take*, tale, time*, tip, top, use*, vote, wave, win, yes*, youngest

PREVIOUSLY TAUGHT SKILLS

as*, at*, be*, go*, he*, hill, in*, is*, it*, on*, up*, we*

■ High-Frequency Words
NEW

its, miss, old, then, what, young

PREVIOUSLY TAUGHT

a, and, are, close, have, said, than, the, to, will

* = High-Frequency Word

BOOK 1 **Not Yet** p. 85

■ Decodable Words

TARGET SKILL: *Initial Blends with l, r, s*

close*, crane, flap, frog, glad, glide, grab, grip, plane, slide, slip, snag, snake, snap, snip, stem, stop*, swim, trot

PREVIOUSLY TAUGHT SKILLS

am*, an*, at*, be*, beg, big*, bit, bite, bone, bug, but*, came*, can*, cannot*, dad, did*, dine, dip, dive, fat*, fed, get*, go*, hole, home*, I*, ice, in*, is*, it*, like*, make*, me*, mice, mom, nab, nice, nip, no*, not*, on*, poke, safe, sit*, take*, tap, time*, tug, up*, us*, until*, we*, yet*, yum, zip

■ High-Frequency Words
NEW

baby, bird, bring, fly, place, she, this

PREVIOUSLY TAUGHT

a, and, best, cold, do, give, left, old, see, small, the, then, to, walk, what, when, will, you

---

BOOK 2 **Big and Small** p. 93

■ Decodable Words

TARGET SKILLS: *Initial Blends with l, r, s; Inflections -s, -es*

bats, boxes, buds, bugs, cactuses, crabs, crane, cranes, dads, dines, flit, flits, foxes, gets*, glad, grab, grabs, homes*, likes*, makes*, moms, nuts, reptiles, runs*, scans, sips, sizes, slugs, snake, snakes, snap, spots, stab, stems, stop*, wades, zips

PREVIOUSLY TAUGHT SKILLS

an*, as*, at*, ate*, be*, big*, bite, box, but*, cage, can*, cannot*, cube, cute, dad, dine, dot, face, fat*, fun*, gave, get*, go*, has*, he*, him*, his*, hole, home*, hop, hot*, hum, ice, if*, in*, inside*, is*, it*, job, kid, like*, man*, men*, mom, mud, name*, nice, not*, on*, pal, pale, pet, quite, run*, safe, same*, sit*, size, up*, use*, yum, zag, zig, zip

■ High-Frequency Words
NEW

baby, bird, birds, blue, bring, fly, her, little, place, this

PREVIOUSLY TAUGHT

a, and, come, find, more, sees, small, the, to, walks, what, will, you